this book belongs to:

COLOR TEST PAGE

DON'T MAKE
ME USE MY
HR
VOICE

IT'S A
HR
THING
YOU'D NOT
UNDERSTAND

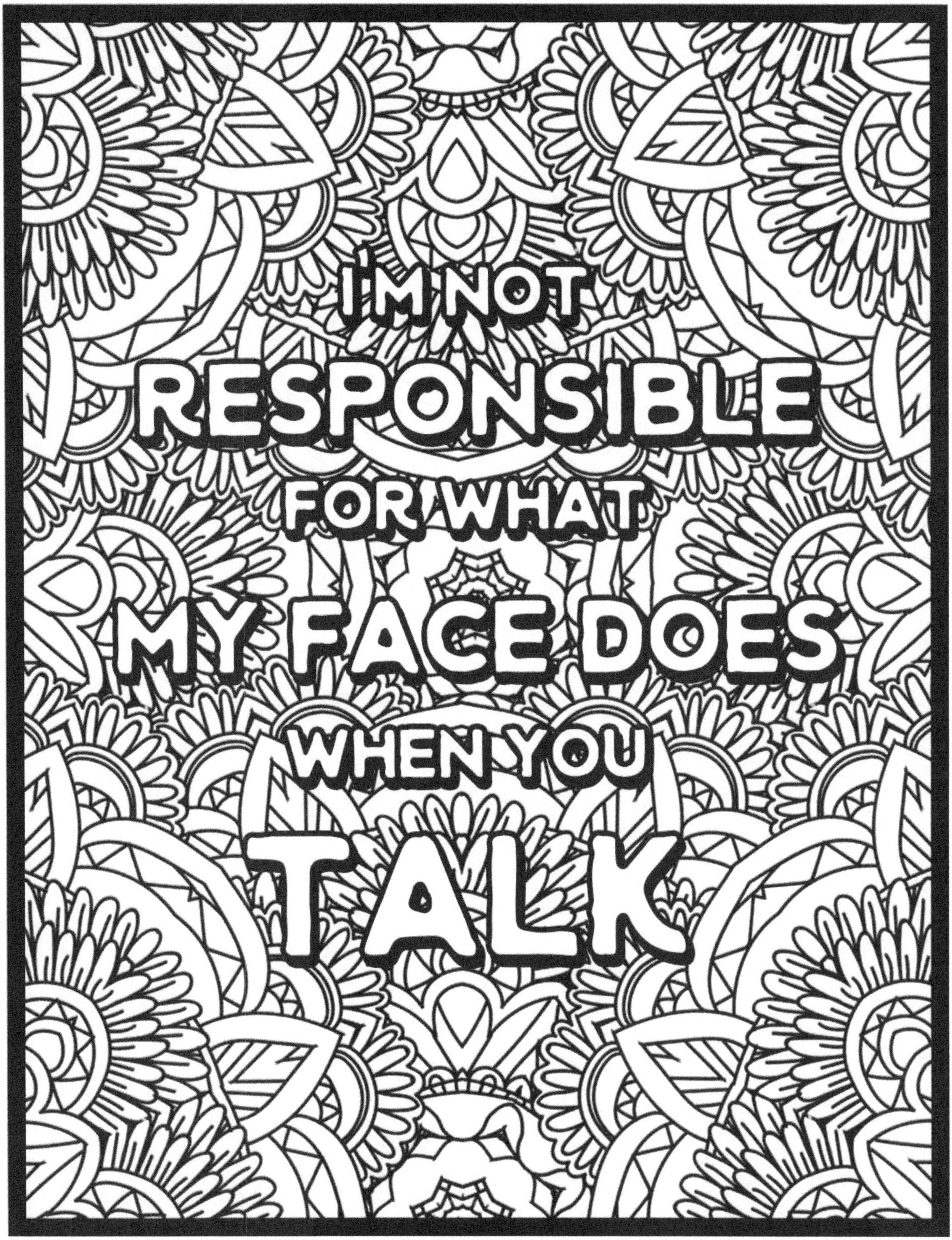
I'M NOT
RESPONSIBLE
FOR WHAT
MY FACE DOES
WHEN YOU
TALK

I WORK IN
HR
TO SAVE TIME
LET'S ASSUME I'M
ALWAYS RIGHT!

52%
BADASS
48%
HUMAN
RESOURCES

MAKE
Today
MAGIICAL

SOME PEOPLE
JUST NEED A
HIGH-FIVE
(IN THE FACE)

Tired-Ass
Human
Resource

FRIDAY.
MY 2ND
FAVORITE
F WORD.

SORRY
I'M DONE
HELPING
ASSHOLES
TODAY

Me
Other
HR

this
HR
is off
Duty

Essential
AF

World's
Okayest
Human
Resource

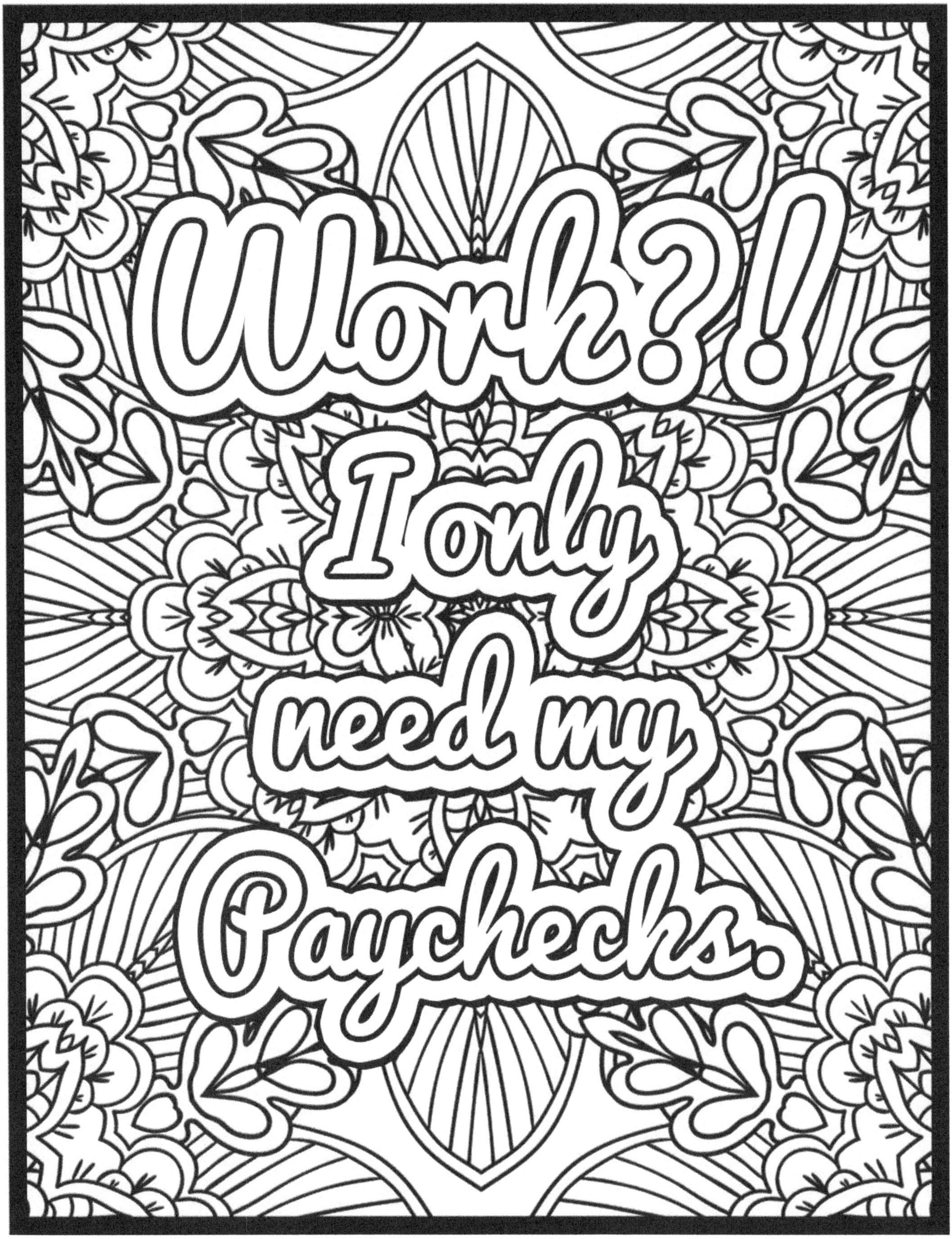
Work?!
I only
need my
Paychecks.

I'm in
HR
What's your
SUPER
POWER?

HUMAN
RESOURCES
BECAUSE
BADASS MIRACLE
WORKER ISN'T AN
OFFICIAL JOB TITLE

I can't fix
Stupid
But I can
Fix what
Stupid
Does

I'm a
Nice Person
Just Don't
Push my
Bitch
Button!

I’VE 101
PROBLEMS
BUT
COLORING
AIN’T ONE